Seymour Simon

EMERGENCY VEHICLES

chronicle books · san francisco

To my grandson Benjamin (Beenie) from Grandpa (Seemie)

Permission to use the following photographs is gratefully acknowledged:

Front cover: © Brand X/PictureQuest; page 1: © Robert Rathe/Getty Images; page 3: © Robert Landau/CORBIS; pages 4–5: © Doreen Levy/Dembinsky Photo Associates; page 6: © Adam Alberti/Dembinsky Photo Associates; pages 8–9: © Digital Vision/Getty Images; pages 10–11: © Jim Regan/Dembinsky Photo Associates; pages 12–13 and back cover © David McNew/Getty Images; pages 14–15: © Peter B. Kaplan/Photo Researchers, Inc.; pages 16–17: © Paul Hardy/CORBIS; page 17 spot and 32: © DiMaggio/Kalish/CORBIS; pages 18–19: © Joseph Pinto/Dembinsky Photo Associates; pages 20–21: © Reuters/CORBIS; pages 22–23: © AFP/Getty Images; pages 24–25: © Pete Saloutos/CORBIS; pages 26–27: © Tom Stewart/CORBIS; pages 28–29: © Jay Silverman Productions/Getty Images; pages 30–31: © Getty Images.

The author especially thanks David Reuther and Ellen Friedman for their thoughtful editorial and design suggestions as well as their enthusiasm for the SeeMore Readers. Also, many thanks to Victoria Rock, Beth Weber, Molly Glover, Tracy Johnson, and Nancy Tran at Chronicle Books for their generous assistance and support of these books.

Book design by E. Friedman.
Typeset in 22-point ITC Century Book.
Manufactured in China.

Library of Congress Cataloging-in-Publication Data
Simon, Seymour.
Emergency vehicles / Seymour Simon.
p. cm.
ISBN-13: 978-0-8118-5406-1 (lib. bdg.)
ISBN-10: 0-8118-5406-X (lib. bdg.)
ISBN-13: 978-8118-5407-8 (pbk.)
ISBN-10: 0-8118-5407-8 (pbk.)
1. Emergency vehicles—Juvenile literature. I. Title.
TL235.8.S56 2006
629.225—dc22
2005014080

Distributed in Canada by Raincoast Books
9050 Shaughnessy Street, Vancouver, British Columbia V6P 6E5

10 9 8 7 6 5 4 3 2 1

Chronicle Books LLC
85 Second Street, San Francisco, California 94105

www.chroniclekids.com

Emergency vehicles are special cars, trucks, airplanes, and boats that help people in trouble.

Fire trucks that shoot water
to put out fires are called fire
engines, or pumpers.

Pumpers can hold about 500 gallons of water.

But for most fires, pumpers get water from fire hydrants.

Ladder trucks carry many kinds of ladders to help rescue people from inside burning buildings. Some of these ladders can reach 100 feet into the air, or about 10 stories high.

Some emergency vehicles carry the Jaws of Life. After a car crash, rescue workers use these cutters to pry the car open and rescue the people trapped inside. They also help get people out of collapsed buildings after earthquakes.

Airport fire trucks carry water as well as special chemicals to help put out fires.

They also carry axes and other tools to help rescue people trapped inside a crashed plane.

Air tankers drop
thousands of gallons
of water onto
wildfires.
The water's red color
is caused by a
chemical added to the
water that helps slow
the flames down.
Tankers also carry
firefighters who
parachute out of
planes to stop blazes.

Fire and rescue boats fight fires on ships and in harbors.

These speedy boats pump thousands of gallons of water each minute.

The water comes from under the boat.

Police cars can drive at high speeds.

They carry two-way radios, first-aid kits, flares, cameras, computers, and lights to direct traffic.

The back seat is used to carry
people who have been arrested.

Armored police trucks are bulletproof on all sides and on the bottom.

Even the windows are bulletproof.

These trucks are used to protect
police from bombs and
dangerous crowds.

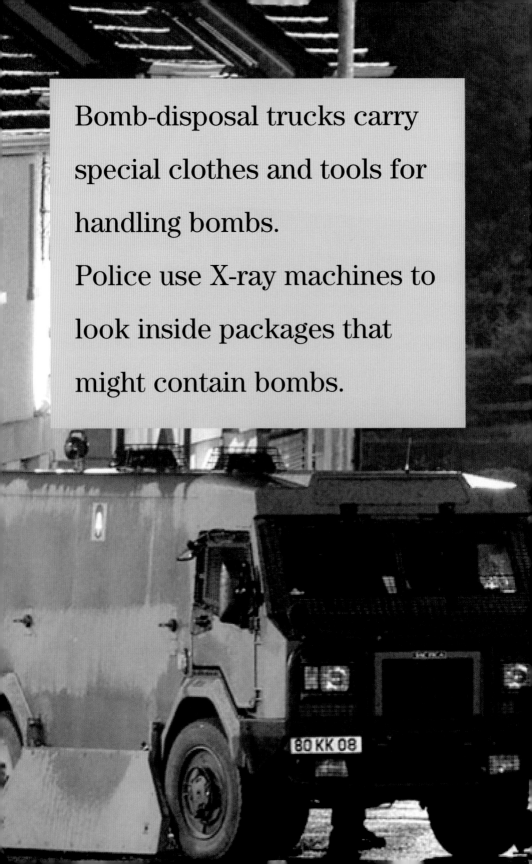

Bomb-disposal trucks carry special clothes and tools for handling bombs.

Police use X-ray machines to look inside packages that might contain bombs.

The trucks also have a special place for carrying bombs to a safe area where they can be exploded.

Police and the military operate bomb-disposal robots by remote control.

These robots have video cameras and long arms. They can go where no person would be safe.

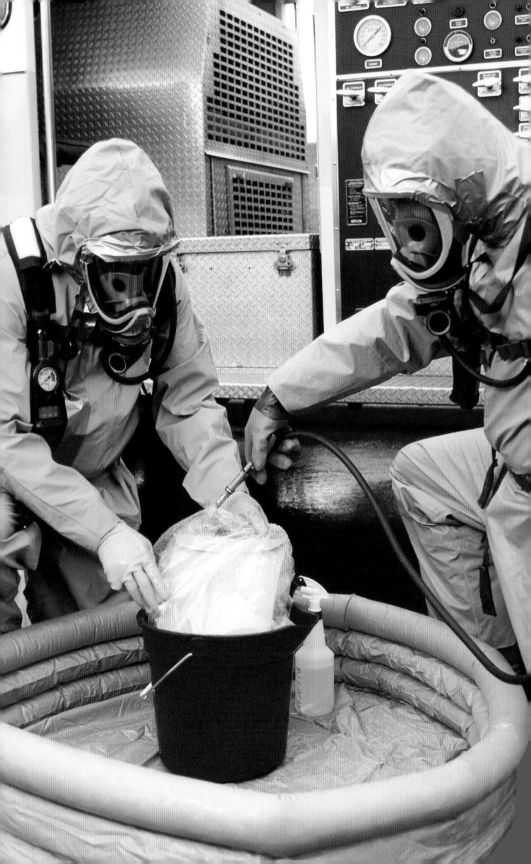

Hazmat trucks carry tools to clean up hazardous chemicals and radioactive wastes. Each truck has computers, a large electric generator, and a command center to direct other emergency vehicles.

Ambulances carry sick or injured people to doctors and hospitals. Ambulances use red flashing lights and a siren to warn other vehicles out of the way.

Medical helicopters carry sick and injured people from remote areas where ambulances cannot go.

Doctors fly onboard the helicopter to treat patients before they reach the hospital.

This is a remote-controlled deep-sea recovery vehicle called *Super Scorpio*. It can dive more than a mile below the surface. It uses cameras and robot arms to get objects from the ocean floor.

Emergency vehicles come in many shapes, sizes, and colors. No matter how they look, emergency vehicles help protect us from all kinds of danger.